Powerful Poems of Overcoming

Dewayne Kendrick

CONTENTS

WARNING TO THE READER

Human behavior is extremely hard to predict seeing as how humans are infinitely unique,

If you are able to decipher the code, you may not receive what you seek.

Some people do not take the time to wonder why others behave in a specific way,

We simply react to surface behavior and accept what others have to say.

This book will open your eyes to a world unseen,

A world where human behavior is triggered by everything.

Once you began to read you will see drama all around,

You will see people in pain, you see people feeling down.

If you find it here, there is nothing to fear, a solution is paired with the issue,

Be sure to discuss the poems that you find as they may not be for you.

Used properly this book can become a powerful tool,

Helping people all around, you are the catalyst to ignite their fuel.

Use this book, enjoy, you may just get a good laugh,

But beware, after you read this book you will walk a new path.

REACH ME

Statement:

Mother, sister, brother, wife, friend, husband, I continue to show up but you are not there,

You won't show me your heart, you won't show me you care.

You act cold and distant but I believe you want to be free,

What am I doing wrong, why won't you open up to me?

I remain strong through the hard times and I really want to help you,

I am doing all I can but still cannot get through.

I am exhausted of trying to help and not getting a return,

My hand is reached out too far and is now starting to burn.

If you care at all, say one little word,

Reach out to me, speak to me, say something I have not heard.

My time is valuable and I want to spend it with you,

If something doesn't change soon, I'll feel like I've done all I can do.

Response:

It is cold, it is dark, and I am all alone,

I feel like the world hates everything I do, everything I do is wrong.

Every time I try I fail, you do not want to be a part of that,

Strangers make fun of me, with their glares and talk behind my back.

You don't want to help me you want to help yourself,

Maybe your energy would be better spent on someone else.

You expect me to come to you but you don't know how I feel,

Walking towards you is like climbing a steep hill.

I cry out for help but no one hears my call,

You say you want to help me until you see me fall.

The room keeps getting smaller as everyone gives up on me,

I've grown used to being alone I call it "doing me".

How can I reach out and grab your hand when I have no hands to reach?

How can I enjoy the sun on a stormy beach?

You are like a floating feather, easy to blow away,

My life is like a raging storm, that is why you cannot stay.

My pain drives everyone away, what makes you so special,

If you want to leave then leave, you would not be the first to do so.

Answer:

You are right, I have not made you a priority,

I have not done all I can do for you to come to me.

That does not mean we should give up, allow me to try again,

I am still here, I will not leave until you let me in.

I am not here for charity, pity, or some false since of obligation,

I am here because I want to be, I truly care, I'm here for the duration.

I will roll down the hill and sit with you at the bottom,

Let me feel your pain so we can conquer it and then some.

Do not worry about strangers, strangers do not worry about you,

Mysteries multiply the pain that you are going through.

You are so special, you have great potential, and an amazing gift,

Your paradigm is your perception, and it is time for a shift.

Let's do this, let's move forward, we will move at a steady pace,

We will not stop, we will not give up, until the pain is banished without a trace.

Aftermath

When helping others in need, people give up when their efforts do not succeed. If the person in need does not respond in the desired manner they are left to their fate. After burning many bridges, these people in need tend to keep to themselves. Every new person that comes around a person in need at this point is looked at as someone who will also eventually give up on them. The question is how do you help someone who seems like they do not want to be helped? We should not expect someone who is sick to cure themselves. If they are able to open up and share their pain they may not be in need in the first place. Basically, people are asking them to cure themselves or be left to rot in their own pain.

If you want to help someone like this first start by feeling their pain. Try your hardest to visualize the pain they are feeling by looking at what you can see from the outside. Do not expect ANYTHING in return for your energy. If the person in need feels like you have something to gain they may believe that you are simply concerned about what you want. Take your time and be genuine with every interaction with them. If you try to rush the person in pain you will once again make it seem that you are rushing because you have some other selfish agenda. Remember that this person has seen many people who were only trying to help them for some self-righteous satisfaction or business agenda. Do not pity the person you want to help, love the person you want to help. Remember the only thing you can do is help a person gain the confidence to help themselves.

CAPTAIN SAVE A WORLD

Statement:

The whole world is suffering, I live in a world full of pain,

How can I enjoy a beautiful day while the homeless freeze in the rain?

Is it my fault? Have I not done enough to contribute to society?

Am I letting people down by mainly being concerned with me?

I feel a heavy burden because I know the world is suffering,

I feel like I can never do enough and I myself am struggling.

How can I get ahead when I take on burdens that are not my own?

I know I can help but helping drags me down.

If I do nothing the guilt will consume me,

If I do too much my inner circles will grow weak.

What is the answer? What do you suggest?

How can I help many and please the rest?

Answer:

The whole world is not suffering, that is a broad statement to make,

Fine tuning your attention on ALL of the pain is a crippling mistake.

Your version of fair is someone else's version of pain, people are infinitely unique,

Do not confuse helping with controlling, and your happiness will peak.

Focus on your immediate world, some things are out of reach,

The ripples you create will spread, passed on for others to teach.

Let your emotional intelligence and mental stability be the sample,

Help yourself first so you can lead by example.

If you take on the burdens of others, then those burdens become your own,

You are not ready for the task if the weight drags you down.

Guilt is a form of self-pity, a dangerous emotion to feel,

You are not helping yourself or anyone else, when your confidence cannot heal.

Trying to please one person involves a very specific program,

Try to please everyone and your mind will begin to jam.

It may be hard at first but do not worry about pleasing everyone,

Be kind to others, love yourself, and the right friends will come.

As for the world, you will play a part in the influence of tomorrow,

Your actions today decide whether you will live in happiness or sorrow.

Be the one to start the chain reaction, become a lighthouse like a star,

Start it in the world you can see, your actions will go far.

Aftermath

Humans are infinitely unique so creating a world where everyone agrees on everything is impossible. People will always make choices that lead them on a specific journey. If you try to "save" everyone all you are really doing is trying to control their will and get them to live in a way that satisfies your own standards.

We live in the world we see every day in our daily routines. We have more power in our own personal worlds because that is where our attention is. If you try to make change to a world you do not give routine attention to than your power will have little control on the change.

If someone hyper focuses on the tragedy in the world and ignores all the positive things happening that person will feel as if the world is doomed. No matter what anyone does there will always be something undesirable happening somewhere. It cannot be avoided due to infinitely different personalities. Focus on issues plaguing the world you live in if you want to make a difference, not the whole world.

I OVERCAME MYSELF

Feeling down, feeling slow, feeling defenseless,
I feel like the walking dead, completely useless.
I am not happy, for now I'm doomed to this state,
My temple, my life, is operating below an average rate.
How did I come to this present, what did I do wrong?
I did not prepare for this day and my defenses are down.
None of that matters, the day is not set,
I will not be defeated by this organic threat.
I will find a way to rise, find a way to break free,
I will find something that will set me free.
Search here search there,
There has to be a remedy, or a cure.
Chanting, rocking, focusing on the issue,
I will overcome, and I will do it with my mental.
The chemicals I need already exist in me,
They can be created on command if I just believe.
My body is powerful, I will not wallow in self-pity,
Think it, feel it, be it, I feel better already.
I made a big fuss over something so small,
I created a powerful sickness from nothing at all.
Am I that weak? Quick to fall, quick to cower,
First sign of danger and so easy to dismiss my power.
No, I am healthy, I am strong,
I make mistakes all day long.
I am not sick, I am not dying!
I am not stuck, I am not lying!
I am power! I feel it in my being,
I will not be destroyed by any means!

Aftermath

Have you ever watched a video of something disgusting and it physically made you sick? Have you ever watched a video of someone doing a good deed and tears started to roll down your face? Has anyone ever given you good news that was so good you begin to get excited and eager? All of these scenarios have something in common, and that is the biological reaction to stimulus coming from a mental change. As humans we have the ability to cause chemical reactions to happen in our bodies just by using mental stimulus. The purpose of this poem is to encourage people to overcome physical sickness in their bodies using mental stimulus as a catalyst. The first step is changing the way you view your situation. See the situation as something you will defeat. The next step is searching like a mad person for a remedy or a cure. Doing this will cause a chain reaction of mental stimulus triggering hope and a mindset of being cured. From this point, your mental state will no longer bind you to the physical sickness that plagues you. The final step is following through with the treatment you discovered.

When it comes to physical treatment there is no telling what you will find and some form of physical treatment is most likely going to be needed. Changing your mental status will make a huge difference but even this is no guarantee of healing. You need to ask yourself where you want to be. Do you want to be the fighter that never gave up and had the highest chance of healing, or do you want to be the depressed, stressed, person who places their life solely in the hands of someone else? If possible, do your own research on top of what anyone else is doing to help you.

Last note. This may not apply to all situations but I find that what you put in your body greatly influences how your body heals. I am talking about food.

LONELINESS

Statement:

There are people all around me.

The people speak to each other, the people call each other's names.

They may laugh, they may argue, they spend time with each other,

As I watch them react to company, I wish to join them, then I think, why bother?

These people do not know me, they walk past me as if I do not exist,

I feel like mist, fading into the air, speaking would be a risk.

Why me? Why must I be alone?

What in my life did I do wrong?

When I speak, people hear but they do not listen,

My words mean nothing, powerlessness, I feel you again.

I am trapped in this loop, and no one will join me,

How do I escape this cycle without someone else's energy?

What do I do specifically?

I do not want some righteous, self-confidence, remedy.

Tell me, step by step, what I am supposed to do,

Here and now, I am reaching out to you.

Answer:

Find something that you love, something you really love to do,

At this thing, there are few better than you.

Set it up, get it ready, then turn on a camera,

Do this thing so amazingly, even you are in aww.

On film, invite people, challenge people, help them do this better,

If you book them they will come, this plan is very clever.

You will make friends, help people, and join a community,

Of like-minded individuals who seek what you seek.

Open your world up, for many people to see,

Let go of pain and insecurities.

When you stood there lonely, did anyone ask you to come?

Did anyone reach out a hand and ask you to join them?

Reach out your hand, you are not the only one,

Be the lighthouse, invite everyone.

People want to join you so do not be afraid,

Step out of the shadows, step out of the shade.

Aftermath

I used to go through flares of depression because no one ever reached out to me. No one ever checked on me, tried to spend time with me, or even needed me for anything. One day I realized that I never checked on anyone, I never tried to spend time with anyone, and I never asked for help from anyone. I expected people to contact me just because I am a friend or a family member. No matter how much you give, no one will ever owe you anything. Do not expect an action to occur without a catalyst. If you do not wish to be lonely create the momentum needed to achieve that goal. Be the one to reach out over and over again. If you are reaching out to the same group of people and not achieving the desired reaction of attention, reach out to a different group of people. Do not try to force anyone to give you attention. Have something to offer, so keeping your company will be a pleasure.

THE BAD PERSON

There are people around me that paint me out to be the enemy,

It started with one moment when I tried to add my energy.

All of a sudden, waves of attacks started to pound me,

Every action I took was looked at as negativity.

People who did not know the whole story joined in to pound me,

No one stood up for me, not even the people who claimed they loved me.

No one will listen, in this moment my words do not matter,

At the core of this attack a few people want to hurt me, pain is what they are after.

My accusers will not hear reason, they will not let anyone think twice,

Others do not realize the true evil, it is calculated and precise.

They want an explosion, after that they can pretend,

That nothing they did was wrong, I am the bad person in the end.

I feel hate and evil bubble beneath my skin,

All I want to do is punish everyone who joined in.

Why am I the only person that can see what is going on here?

Why are people so quick to throw away my whole character?

Oh well, you want me to show the pain that I have stored?

You want me to release my frustration and be stoned by the horde?

You got it, let me give you what you desire,

Hate, anger, and evil, all these things are required.

If I am the bad person I will show you how bad I can be,

In time the mistake you made today will be revealed for everyone to see.

Inner voice response:

If you are angry you do not have control,

You are not disciplined, you are not whole.

Instead of releasing anger and hate,

Remove yourself from situation and leave them to fate.

People who insight anger and pain,

Carry the most pain and desire company to remain sane.

Do not lose yourself, hold on to your composure,

Remove the energy from your world and that conflict will be over.

You are not the bad person people make you out to be,

Invest more time into loving yourself and you will not break so easily.

Aftermath

There are many factors that take place when confrontation occurs. These many factors are often overlooked in the moment of the confrontation. When you explore other potential factors in a confrontation, a world of choices opens up on how to handle the situation. Some options may work better than others but there is one option that rarely ever works. The one option that rarely works is turning to anger and hate. Have you ever made any decisions out of anger? If so how well did those decisions turn out? When humans experience intense emotions they often make decisions without thinking about the consequences of their actions. Sometimes people do think about the consequences, intense emotion temporarily numbs the thoughts of grief the decision will bring. If you love yourself no one will be able to push you to a place where you attempt to hurt others.

If we could all see everything that every person has ever done we might label most adults as "bad people". Understand that we are infinitely unique so humans will never completely agree on all things. Keep a healthy distance from people who do things that you are not strong enough to overcome. Build your strength so that when you face these people again they cannot control you. When you are so high strung that everything seems like an attack, you are weak and need to get stronger. Verbal attacks cannot penetrate your mental stability when you are confident and aware of human nature. If you are ever considered a bad person respect the OPINION of the people who labeled you as such and remove yourself from that dimension.

INVISIBLE BARRIER

Why won't I do the things I know I need to do?

Why do I say things I know are not true?

 I want to do this and I want to do that,

I dream of doing this and I dream of doing that.

Action for satisfaction eludes me,

Time and dedication do not come easy.

So, I have the knowledge and the wisdom needed to rise,

But I stare at opportunity in confusion, and watch it pass by.

Oh wait, I know the reason why,

I know the reason why I watch life pass me by.

I do not believe it is possible for me to live on high,

I cannot visualize my success, no matter how hard I try.

That is the factor that holds me down,

That is what stops me in my tracts and keeps me on the ground.

Now that I know what the enemy looks like, I can defeat myself,

I know my own strengths and weaknesses better than anyone else.

It took long enough but better late than never,

I will turn the key, unlock the door, and hold it open forever.

Aftermath

No matter what outside source you try to blame for your current condition the ultimate responsibility for your condition falls to you. Knowing the responsibility is yours is not enough to drive you to your destination. You must truly believe that it is possible for the goal to be achieved. Humans are always trying to secure and predict the future. We cannot secure and predict the exact future but we can visualize what we want to happen and guide ourselves as close to that prediction as possible in our everyday lives. Defeat yourself by destroying the invisible barriers your personal traits have created. Just a heads up, improvement of the self never ends. As you grow there will always be new personal barriers to destroy. Prioritize on destroying the specific barriers that block the short-term goals you are trying to achieve in the moment.

SO HAPPY

I'm just so darn happy, how do I keep this thing going?

How do I keep the smile on my face and the positive energy flowing?

People, I need people, together energies combine,

Building momentum, we are so happy, it is about time.

Hold on there is an acquaintance with negative energy,

Negative energy so powerful they need to get away from me.

Whew that was a close one, time to move on,

Misery loves company and misery is strong.

Normally I try to overpower negative in my life,

But today I feel so good, I dodge the fight.

What a wonderful day to be alive,

This is not how to live, it is how to thrive.

A nice cold beverage, something hot to eat, that would do me right,

Fresh air, new scenery, and a little sunlight.

Oh yea, this feels so good, I knew I could keep this going,

Energy, energy, energy, positive energy flowing.

Payday, the weekend, early morning breakfast,

Whatever got me to this point I need not forget it.

I want to trigger it again, every day if need be,

I will find the stimulation, document it, and let that be a key.

Aftermath

A "peak experience" describes a feeling of total happiness. When you are so happy you feel like a child playing, without a care in the world. Feeling this happy is rare for many people and even hard to achieve. Think of the happiest moments you have had. Put them together and find what connects all of those moments and you will have a clue on finding what makes you as an individual happy.

Think of happiness as a bright glowing energy that radiates around your body. When someone comes around with the same bright glowing energy, it may be powerful enough to transform your happiness energy to anger or sadness. It is ok to dodge the fight every now and then to enjoy a moment of total happiness.

THE POWER OF SLEEP

I work the grave shift and I am so tired,

But as soon as it is time to get off, the sun comes up and I am wired.

I try to go to sleep but only sleep for a few hours,

I toss, I turn, and I wake up feeling sour.

I know I need my rest but there are too many things to do,

Besides, when I try to sleep I get distracted by you.

It is torture being tired at work,

I feel like a zombie and I act like a jerk.

How do I find a balance when I know that I am wrong?

How do I fix a problem, when I have known the answer all along?

Sleep, sleep is what I really need,

Understanding how much it affects me will help me succeed.

If I respect sleep and give it the value it deserves,

I will plan my day around it, not forgetting or losing my nerve.

Now I see the change rest brings,

The poise, the presence, and the energy to do things.

I recommend everyone find a way,

To do one of the most important things you will do in a day.

Aftermath

We sabotage our bodies productivity levels when we do not allow our bodies to receive enough rest. If you have the luxury of sleeping whenever your body gets tired I would recommend that but for others who need their bodies to perform at very specific times I would recommend making sleep a high priority. Most people understand how important sleep is yet they still do not get enough of it. Let this poem be a reminder to you or someone you know. Allow this poem to be the catalyst to a more enjoyable, fulfilling day because you were able to sleep until your body was satisfied.

THE UNFORGIVEN

After I am angry I am sad and hurt by the decisions I made,

I regret my actions all together and I feel like a monster.

All I want to do is apologize over and over until I cannot breathe,

I want to give all of myself for the pain that I have caused.

There is no escape, I was wrong, I see that clearly,

I am totally powerless because I feel so guilty.

Whatever punishment falls upon me I will not resist,

I will never forgive myself, for this.

(if you have not forgiven yourself, this is where you stop)

Time Goes by

I forgave myself after all,

How long could I live in sorrow, how far down could I fall?

I will never forget and I still wish I could change the past,

But I could no longer live in pain, anymore and I would be dead.

On rock bottom there is nowhere else to fall,

You either get up and stand tall, or you do not get up at all.

If you have not forgiven me I hope you find peace,

A grudge is like a cyclone of pain that will not cease.

If you have forgiven me I am happy you moved on,

I pray for love in your heart, I hope you remain strong.

Aftermath

Sometimes in the middle of anger people lose themselves in the anger. It is not uncommon for people to regain consciousness after the tirade is over. Anger is a powerful emotion that will cause people to do things they regret. Unfortunately, the victim on the receiving end of the anger is placed with a hard choice to forgive the person or hold a grudge. Sometimes the victim wishes that the attacker will never have peace. The victim often uses the incident to bring pain to the attacker. No matter who will or will not forgive, it is important to forgive yourself. Allow yourself to live a fulfilling life without beating yourself up because someone will not forgive you.

BEFORE WE BECOME WE

Before we become we, I must become me,

Happiness, peace, and love all included.

I want to love you and give you all that I have,

First, I need to invest into myself so I have something to give.

I know that I am constantly learning and changing,

But currently I am not mentally ready for rearranging.

I know this because I feel hesitation,

I want to give you all of me without reservation.

I cannot love you if I do not fully love me,

I am not saying that I have low self-esteem.

I need to find my way, sometimes I feel confused,

On who I am and what I am going to do.

Sometimes I am insecure, sometimes I doubt my power,

Sometimes this world makes me want to hide and cower.

I am not sending you away, I am not saying we cannot spend time,

I am saying before we become one I must mature to my prime.

You are strong, you are ready, and I believe that you love me,

I will get stronger, I will be ready, my actions are open for you to see.

If I understand me there will be less confusion in the fusion of you and I,

I will know that I am ready when the time is right.

I want our relationship to be powerful, roots thicker than a full-grown tree,

My goal is not just to date you, I want holy matrimony.

You may believe that what I am saying is all about me,

When we join together we become we.

My issues will leak into our everyday lives,

I will become a burden, you may grow to despise.

Help me by loving me and trusting my choice,

Support me, continue to be there for me, and here my voice.

There are things that I love to do, things we can explore,

There are habits that I must release, I do not want anymore.

There are people I must cut off, our personalities do not mix,

There are people I must forgive; the grudge feels like dragging bricks.

Finances distract my focus, I must secure my routine,

I do not want to be too concerned with where we get our green.

Before I give you the keys,

There are some issues I must resolve to put my mind at ease.

Until then, I promise to continue to be me,

The one you are attracted to, the one you love to see.

I will never give you less, I will always give you more,

I will not make loving me transform into a chore.

Before we become we, I must become me,

Happiness, peace, and love all included.

Aftermath

Buckle your seatbelt before you try to help anyone else buckle theirs. You must love yourself before you can properly love anyone else. This does not mean a special person cannot join the journey to self-love, but that person must be patient. Many relationships fail because of insecurity and lack of confidence coming from an individual who is not familiar with their own being.

BEWARE THE DELIGHTED SELFISH ONE

In a relationship of any kind people give and they receive. Giving and receiving will never change in a relationship, though the content of what is shared may change. Beware the delighted selfish one who loves what you give. This person loves what you give but you do not love what you receive back from this person. When you try to make an adjustment so that you too can be delighted, that alters the delight of the selfish one. When you alter the delight of the selfish one, the selfish one becomes agitated and possibly angry. If you stop giving to the Delighted Selfish One (DSO) do not be surprised at the response you receive. You see, just because you were in pain or not receiving what you wanted, it is still not enough reason for you to take your gifts elsewhere in the eyes of the DSO. With the DSO, it is all about getting what they want. The DSO does not care that you were not getting what you wanted. The DSO is like a baby with a pacifier in his/her mouth, once you take out the pacifier he/she cries. The DSO smites and blames you for being a horrible person. Being truthful is not good enough for the DSO. Was there ever a time you could say you are not interested in what someone else is giving and they NOT blow up on you? Human beings can be so selfish, only caring about what they are getting. Beware the delighted selfish one. This one is hard to spot. Establish clear communication from the beginning of a relationship, although even this may not stop the DSO's rampage.

Aftermath

If you are under fire from a DSO there is a simple way to free yourself of this drama. Pretend that the DSO is not in your life and be yourself the best way you can. Love yourself and tend to your own specific needs. Do not respond to the attention seeking, manipulative, selfish power of the DSO. One of two things will happen when you do this; either the DSO will respond with a humble attitude (if this happens make it clear what energy you desire) or the DSO will remove themselves from your life. It may be necessary for you to find a way to completely remove yourself from the situation. If you need to remove yourself stay removed. Going back will only make the DSO stronger.

COMPETITION FOR A JOB

I remain silent, my senses are enhanced,

Watching movement, hearing voices, studying every glance.

Smiles all around, happy people don't stand in my way,

You are not my friends, strip the facade, you are my enemy today.

We compete for the same meal and eat at the same table,

You will not understand me; I will not give you a label.

I understand my weakness, you will try to find,

I am far ahead of you and you will see that in due time.

People dress like this, people dress like that,

I'm not focused on what you're wearing, I trim the fat.

I see the goal ahead of me, I have tunnel vision,

You cannot break my drive or sway my attention.

I will break this position open and show everyone I am the best,

Claim you can challenge me and I will put you to the test.

I am 50 feet high; a great being sits in the room,

If it's between me and you, then that means your doom.

Aftermath

When you go into an interview for a job or you are in competition for a raise with fellow employees, everyone wishes each other good luck. While you are waiting for your interview other candidates smile in your face and act as if you are friends. Coworkers, teammates (competing for the same position), jobseekers, and even students compete to be the best. Losing is not fun nor profitable in these scenarios. Do not let kind, well spoken, well dressed, smiling competition get the upper hand by pretending to be your friend.

DRAMA

We all look for passion and love but instead we find drama,

People that say and do hurtful things causing pain and trauma.

We latch on to the drama because it is a source of attention,

We create more drama to keep it going and tighten the tension.

Did I mention, people who create drama are lonely from lack of attention,

Lack of love, lack of passion, feeling restricted like detention.

We fear good feelings will not last,

So, we sabotage the positive to protect ourselves from the blast.

Drama is contagious, just like love and happiness,

Competition is merciless on who is the best.

If you find that you are spreading information about the next person,

If you catch yourself feeling childish in every situation.

You may be spreading drama, it is best not to be the one,

Drama can turn into hate, and hate is no fun.

Aftermath

Be careful not to bring painful drama into your world. Drama is contagious and sometimes people do not realize that they are contributing to the spreading of it. Watch out for people who use clever ways to pull you into the drama. Simply asking for your opinion is enough to pull you into the drama. Work on giving more focus to solutions instead of harping on the same subject back and forth achieving no movement or resolution. If people want to go on and on about the same drama that is a key indicator that this person feeds off of the attention received from that subject.

KTP MINOR (ALL ANGLES)

Are you finding it hard to accomplish your goals?

Do you procrastinate until your plan is filled with holes?

Maybe you have tried many times to no avail,

And now you have given up on the largest scale.

Let me inform you of a tool that will help you rule,

A tool that will ensure you succeed no matter the odds.

Angle.

If a square piece does not fit into a circle hole you must try another shape,

If you give up with the square than that is your fate.

Try another angle and keep changing angles until one angle fits,

Try all angels until you accomplish it.

You can use math and you can plan,

Trying all angles covers the span.

Stop, think, breath and relax,

In armor there are always cracks.

Keep pushing until you get in,

If you want it bad enough you will have it in the end.

Aftermath

KTP is an acronym for Keys to Power. This poem is designed to open your eyes to new possibilities. If you try to do something and you fail to do it, do not give up. Try doing the same thing but using a different method to do it. Consider the possibility that you have not put enough energy into the task, therefore it cannot be accomplished. Adding more energy to the task is just another example of trying a different angle. No one strategy is guaranteed to work every time. Try everything! Empty the entire clip on one target! Give it all that you have and then give it all that you don't have. If you want it bad enough you will have it in the end.

THE BREAK UP

Statement:

Your energy has been ripped away from my energy.

The impact of such a large gap in my life is catastrophic.

My world begins to crumble in an effort to reach out for the energy it is used to,

This feels like going cold turkey off of a highly addictive drug, so painful.

I begin to search for your energy, but without you, it does not exist,

The only solution is going back to the energy that harmed me before.

The only solution is trying to get you back.

Your energy strikes my world but I have grown numb to the pain.

Your energy is refreshing because it is predictable and consistent.

There is no amount of inner strength to prepare for this big of a change in my life.

I am running out of options,

I need you, I miss you, but I do not want you.

Every second that passes my world becomes darker, crumbling because it is missing something.

Is there no other way?

I could find someone else,

But that person is quickly discarded because that person is not you.

I see no answer, I see no way, what am I to do?

What am I to do?

Answer:

Addictions are easier to replace than destroy.

Trying to destroy muscle memory and mental memory is like swimming against a rip current, you get tired and eventually the current will carry you where it will.

Become as active as possible to find a new routine,

Join a club, group, or team.

Do something new consistently,

The new challenge will alleviate the pain.

The physical and mental effort will absorb the energy you used grieving over the loss of someone else's energy.

Expand the energy you have within yourself.

Before any energy enters your world, there is your energy.

Rediscover yourself.

Unlock the clamps, set the painful energy free,

It may come back transformed, on its own will, if it was meant to be.

In a world where you place painful energy above,

You live in the world you are thinking of.

Let it go, love yourself, become active and you will see,

What it is like to be free, of someone else's energy.

Aftermath

There is one thing tragedy has in common that people fear. That one thing is an unpredictable future. Humans love to feel like they have a hold on the future. People act based on what they believe the outcome of their actions will be. People who are in relationships with each other share energy. The majority of their lives are spent with each other. If you remove one person, the entire routine of both people will collapse and the future will be hard to predict.

Remember that before you were in a relationship you were whole. You had a life before the relationship and you will have one after the relationship. Build up your own energy to bridge the gap where the other person's energy was. Love yourself and enjoy life in your own way. Go back to loving yourself like you should have been doing the entire time. If you love yourself, being with yourself should not be so dreadful.

PETTY SHIRT

You've made your point you've made your move, now which route will I choose.

I have played this game time and time again, ye old petty shirt, you will not win.

You come from friends, you come from foes, you come from people I barely know.

You seek attention or maybe you don't, ye old petty shirt, this time I won't.

Tether me down from the inside out, an endless sea of questions covered by a cloud?

A simple turn of the head, and you go away, ye old petty shirt, I will not play.

Normally I would scream, sometimes I would shout, I'd even go far to point you out.

I'd waste so much energy showing everyone you are there, ye old petty shirt, this time I do not care.

I love myself I love my life, I am so fulfilled, things are so right.

So many wonderful things I see every day, ye old petty shirt, you seem small to me.

Let me vanquish your negativity with some love and respect,

Let me vanquish your existence with some good old neglect.

At this point you have no power over me, sheesh, what a waste of energy.

Oh well, I just wanted to let you know, you mean nothing to me, you are not my foe.

As for me I have bigger fish to fry, ye old petty shirt, farewell and good bye.

Aftermath

Some people take pride in being petty. Some people believe being petty is an art and they enjoy the craft. People who are petty get enjoyment out of belittling people. If you are on the receiving end of petty shirt this poem gives an insight on how to defeat the negative feelings and reactions that may come after an attack. Do not feed your attacker with attention. Let the petty shirt suffocate, as it needs your attention to breathe. If you cannot overcome the petty shirt it is a testimony to your level of mental stability. Confidence is another major factor that will help you overcome the petty shirt. If you love yourself, petty shirt will appear as a desperate cry for help from your attacker, or an attempt to be a comedian.

STRANGER WHO ARE YOU

I do not understand your world; will it benefit me if I try?

Are you going to be in my life long enough for me to care if you lie?

Maybe, maybe not, if I'm asking you have my attention,

Ask yourself the same question about me; tell me, what is your intention?

My circle is not perfect, I am missing some pieces,

I will judge you based on how fast my tolerance of you increases.

You have knocked on my door and I am reluctant to let you in,

Please excuse my caution; this is a dangerous world we live in.

We are all very special but sometimes we do not match,

Put together we form negative energy and I do not want to deal with that.

You may want what I can give, but do you have something for me?

I'll take positive energy coming from your personality.

Stranger who are you? I don't need to know your back story,

Who are you today, filled with drama or filled with glory.

Aftermath

Relationships always start with two strangers meeting each other. We try to put our best foot forward but we know eventually another side will emerge. Wouldn't it be nice if we could fast forward to get a glimpse of that other side before we decided to let a stranger into our worlds? When someone new comes around we are cautious because we have had bad experiences with people in previous relationships. In the beginning of a relationship I believe we doom ourselves to repeat the past because we tell stories of the past. Instead of learning a lesson we recreate our pain by bringing the memories back and reinforcing the trauma. Instead of speaking about everything that has happened in the past, we should focus on talking about who we think we are today. Stranger who are you? Now. This will help both people look forward to the stated qualities. If you do not know who you are today make it a priority to understand yourself. Not knowing who you are is like flying a plane without a pilot. It does not allow you to strategically work towards happiness.

WHY I AM SO GOOD

I will not stop, unless I cannot move,

I will not give up, I cannot lose.

My power does not only lie within me,

My power is in everything you see.

The drive that propels me to live and love life,

Is life itself which is powerful in its own right.

Living life to the fullest and being happy brings a feeling I truly treasure,

If you have not felt this feeling you must know it is a feeling you cannot measure.

In my world it is not wrong or foul,

To live for moments, to live for now.

So, I will continue to live for today and tomorrow,

I will rise above those who live in sorrow.

My energy overpowers the negative and the weak,

My words have power and meaning every time I speak.

So today, this morning, I hereby declare,

To never give up, until I get there.

Aftermath

This poem is about loving yourself and making a conscious effort to enjoy life. We live in a sea of humans who do not have enough love for themselves as individuals. When you love yourself, you stand out, and the sea of "living zombies" (humans) tries to pull you back to a state that matches the overall energy. Everyone desires some form of power. The power to help homeless individuals, the power to maintain a family, the power to contribute to society and more. Every action we take requires power of some kind. When you are powerful in your own world the world itself becomes your power. The people that love you, the connections you have made, the money energy you have accumulated and more. Everyone is unique so living life to the fullest will always look different per person. Living for today is amazing and there is nothing wrong with also planning for tomorrow. The "self" is the largest hurdle you will face but beware of those who live in sorrow. You must transform their hurtful energy into love energy or avoid them completely. Even knowing that nothing is promised or guaranteed, I will die trying or succeed.

WHY AM I HERE?

Statement:

I want to know why I am here,

What is my purpose, and why do I care?

Who can tell me why I am here?

Who can dig deep inside my heart and find what's in there?

A psychologist may be able to help me dig it out,

A close family member may know what I am talking about.

But none of them will ever come close,

To finding what I desire most.

Someone told me that the one is me,

To find my inner most desires, to help me see.

I do not understand how I can be the one,

I have not been taught, my journey has just begun.

People talk all day but no one will grab my hand,

Someone please help me, where do I begin?

Answer:

I hear you, I acknowledge your existence, and yes, I feel your pain,

I was once unsure of myself, my wisdom is yours to gain.

Knowledge turns into wisdom, wisdom helps you live,

You need to educate yourself to find out what you have to give.

Read psychology books to get an idea of human reactions,

Understanding human behavior will help you get some traction.

Recall in your mind, your happiest times, take notes of what you were doing,

Strip the memories down to the bone, to see what you are pursuing.

Family fun, the love of someone special, or maybe peace and solitude,

Don't miss anything when dissecting the memory, be sure to stay true.

Purpose is unique to every individual that is why only you can find it,

Beware of individuals who will try to capture and bind it.

Distractions are everywhere so meditation is a major key,

Meditate every day and it will help set you free.

Everyone has unique abilities, using them helps you feel whole,

People are always changing and sometimes get lost in the old.

Do not use a pre-created personality to find what you hold dear,

Love yourself, explore yourself, and you will find why you are here.

Aftermath

This poem is meant to help people discover some form of purpose in life. Sometimes people feel like they are going thru the motions of life without actually living it. Sometimes people feel like they are living too much and not even doing what they truly want to be doing. The answers concerning self-purpose can only come from within. I can use my influence to guide you along the path to self-discovery but no one knows you like you know yourself. I can expose some barriers that may be blocking your path, I can hold your hand and walk with you along your journey, I cannot put you on my back and walk for you. Why are you here? You are here to live. You will die, but you are alive to live. Finding purpose will allow you to use your many gifts in such a way that will bring you joy. Purpose can change and there can be more than one purpose per person. Use the steps in this poem to find your purpose and thrive in life.

PLAN B

I tried to do it alone and I spun my wheels.

The narrow tunnel my thought path created gave me no ideas.

All my knowledge and wisdom did me little good in this place,

My will power alone was not enough to keep pace.

I saw a hand and I was reluctant to grab it,

This meant a blow to my pride and I could not have that.

This hand was cold and had betrayed me before,

It had betrayed me and I will not allow it to do that once more.

All other hands teased me with future promises,

Promises that were kept out of reach unless I had the resources.

This cold hand was as low as me,

It offered a small amount of security.

So, I grabbed it, I grabbed the cold hand,

Instantly my tunnel vision opened up again.

I saw a new way, I saw a new light,

My engines were restarted, I was ready to fight.

All it took was someone else's energy,

To change my world, to help me see.

Aftermath

When we have been hurt by someone before it is hard to go back to that person for help. Some people would rather struggle alone than ask for help from someone they know will harm them. Keep the goal in perspective and if that cold hand is the only hand willing to offer the help you need, grab it. Understand the issues that come with grabbing that hand and use the momentum created to move on quickly. It is better to receive help and relief from someone you do not like than to wallow in pain until a new hand comes along.

PAYDAY

It's payday and I just got paid,

I get excited thinking about the things I am going to do today.

Of course, I will pay my bills, get that out of the way,

After that the rest is mine! It is time to play.

Bowling, movies, I need some fast food,

I have been broke all week, and not in a good mood.

You know what? Let's hit the bar, drinks are on me,

I just bought some new clothes and I want to show them off you see.

I love payday, it makes me feel good,

Money is the cane I lean on, more than I should.

When I have money I feel alive,

When I do not have money, I feel deprived.

But less talk, more spending, I feel a little down,

Time to hit my favorite restaurant at the end of town.

How much do I have left? Let me take a little peak,

Oh no I'm flat broke, in the middle of the week.

I just got paid, my pockets must have a leak,

Oh yea, little by little I spent all my money thru the week.

My money cane is gone, I can barely move,

Once again, I am in a bad mood.

I feel so stupid, I should have saved my money,

I hope I do not take my frustration out on the people around me.

Yes!!

It's payday and I just got paid,

I get excited thinking about the things I am going to do today,

Of course, I will pay my bills, get that out of the way,

After that the rest is mine! It is time to, **save**.

Aftermath

When you feel helpless you feel powerless. If you feel like you can barely afford to buy food you will have a constant worry in your mind. No matter what you are doing you will feel the agitation in the back of your mind and you may be worried about doing anything that may cost money. A simple short-term solution is to save a paycheck or two so you will always have a buffer. Create a budget so you are not randomly spending your money. A budget can be as simple as breaking your paycheck up into categories (survival money, play money). Feeling down because you do not have any money is something that can be helped with a lifestyle change, it does not need to contribute to the list of issues you have to overcome.

I SEE YOU

A new person is preparing to enter into my daily routine,

I enjoy meeting new people and interacting with the energy they bring.

This new person is different from the rest,

I can feel what is coming and it is not for the best.

This is the same energy that I felt before,

When the energy of another tried to tear down my door.

I see the cogs turning and the energy rearing back,

Latching itself into place and preparing for an attack.

Bring it on.

I do not now and never again will I live my life in fear,

I have prepared myself for times like this and my objectives are clear.

I love myself and the people in my life, my inner most circle is strong,

When the attack comes and my world is the target, I will not be alone.

No matter what form the attack comes in, I know it does not stand a chance,

In order to succeed the attack must destroy my confidence.

I will not deviate from my goals or my purpose,

I will not abandon my values or sellout to the first purchase.

To the person at my door, I will not try to stop you, come test my frequency,

Join my flow, and be surrounded by my energy.

You may like the taste, and instead of fight you just might want to join me,

If that is the case then you are welcome, I will treat you like family.

Aftermath

When someone becomes a part of your daily routine that persons energy is added into your world. The amount of energy (influence) varies but it will be there. Speaking, eye movements, body language, openness, and many more triggers stimulate a collective vibe you will get from the person. This poem is meant to illuminate and isolate that feeling you get when you meet someone new. This poem is also meant to let the new person know that you see them, you are open to peace, and ready for war. Most times the best way to snuff out harmful energy is to starve it by not feeding it your attention. There will always be unexpected issues when change happens, knowing that they are coming will help you prepare for them.

If you are faced with a situation where you cannot remove yourself from harmful energy the only option is to extinguish the harmful energy. Let it rain! Shower the harmful energy with your own love energy. What does that look like? Be kind, and do not rush to judgement. Trust the person with task that let the person know you are giving them trust, they can earn it later. Do not ask too many questions. Allow the person a chance to learn the ways of the new environment. Be patient with the person when they do something that may be harmful to your world. Another way to remove the energy is to expose it to other people whose energies are also in your world. For this to work you must still be kind to the person. If your kindness is consistent and genuine others will notice any attacks from the other person's energy. The key is being consistent and genuine with your kindness. Do not talk behind the person's back even if your friends are doing so. If your friends transform and begin to bring harmful energy to you when they did not before, talk to them. Do not bring up the new person, just talk to them as friends. If they are your friends they will hear you and acknowledge your pain. With all eyes on the new person, that person will either leave or conform. This does not mean the person has to become someone else, it just means that while in the presence of this group, that person will act accordingly.

I AM LEGEND

What is a legend? I'm a legend, I will live on forever,

In the hearts and minds of those who remember.

I will influence and train men and women to be greater,

In passing on knowledge I receive pleasure.

Meaning and purpose are a common goal for all,

Fulfilling my purpose helps me stand tall.

My purpose is manifested from the life that I have lived,

I recognize my heart's desire and neediness to give.

How did I truly become a legend?

I found a way to look through the blurry fog of life.

I found the meaning of my own life and charged toward the end,

It was a long ride filled with broken hearts I could not mend.

I could taste the end, so I could feel the beginning,

That there was no end to my wonderful feeling.

I became legend once I woke from the matrix,

Being one of few who ever made it.

No matter how small the aspect may be,

Growth will continue within me.

I am a legend because I bring people with me,

Side by side we set each other free.

I have followed and have been led to an undesirable place,

I have followed and have been led to a space filled with grace.

Now I lead and for those who follow,

You stand beside me today and tomorrow.

Aftermath

In this poem a legend is someone that has realized the true meaning of his/her individual life through trial and error. According to this poem a legend is also someone who has become a major influence in the lives of those who follow him/her. Become your own version of a legend. Become the greatest version of yourself (whatever that may be). Doing this will significantly increase your satisfaction with the life you are living and you will become an influence to those who are willing to follow your example in your world.

HELP MYSELF

People say you are not alone and you should not be ashamed to ask for help.

I have reached out and asked for help.

I have humbled myself, put my heart on a platter to be devoured or healed,

I have taken my pride, locked it away, tight and sealed.

The help I received was sarcasm and side glares,

Chitter chat behind my back and bitter stares.

Maybe it is a job or maybe they feel guilty,

Maybe a power high or maybe something I can't see.

All I know is this help I do not want, it makes me feel worse than before,

This help makes me feel like an ungrateful peasant, always asking for more.

I am sent in circles, chasing my own tail,

Anything to belittle my presence, my mind is brittle and frail.

I am watching you now, before I was not,

I was excited at first for the chance at another shot.

Using your help, you now own me,

I do what I must to not step on your toes and keep you happy.

I swallow my opinion and forfeit any rights,

Then I am rolled over and treated like a parasite.

But wait, what is this? A light I have found,

Real help does exist and it is all around.

Help that feels, help that loves, help that truly cares,

Help that smiles, help that understands, and really wants me to get there.

I almost gave up on my goal; I thought I was doomed to fail,

I thought I had tried everything to climb out the well.

If you feel like you are in a worse place than before,

You need to find new help; you need to find the door.

Aftermath

Many times, we need help from others to move forward. People are always saying do not be afraid to ask for help. The energy that comes with the help is what people fear. Has anyone ever belittled you because they helped you and now they feel as if they can talk to you like you are beneath them? Has anyone ever helped you and then tried to control you because they feel you owe it to them after receiving their help? Sometimes you may feel as if your presence is a burden while receiving help from someone. I just want you to know that there are always options. Never believe that there is nothing else you can do. Put yourself out there and let the world know you need help. There is someone out there looking to help a person with your circumstances and will truly be delighted by your success. The key is being kind and humble to all people. It is easy to turn someone who originally wanted to help you into someone who cannot wait to get rid of you.

GUARD UP

No matter the situation if there is a goal there should be a guard.

A guard provides the agitation for growth towards the goal.

Has anyone ever asked you to let down your guard?

When your guard is up it is hard for others to play their card.

Everyone has intentions and motivations to achieve,

If your guard stands in the way of someone else's motives they will need that guard relieved.

If your guard is up that is a sign that something else is required,

For you to lower it on your own time or whenever it is desired.

There is a guard for every situation, one person can have many guards,

If you do not have a guard create one and it will help you work hard.

When you get a new job the first few months you feel you must prove your worth,

You prove your worth, drop your guard, and feel like you are on home turf.

Now that your guard is down you feel like your coworkers are your best friends,

You tell them about your personal life, you talk of latest trends.

But there was someone watching you, jealous of your success,

Waiting for you to drop your guard to make your life a mess.

Now your information is out and a weakness they have found,

You have opened the door for drama to pin you to the ground.

The same scenario applies in many different ways,

Your guard protects your will, and it never betrays.

If you miss out on something because of your guard then you were not ready,

When it is time to remove your guard, the process is easy and steady.

Aftermath

There will always be barriers to your goals and forces set to dismantle any progress you have made towards your goals. Imagine being under attack and not knowing you are under attack. That is like a leech sucking out all of your blood while you grow weaker and weaker, all the while you do not understand why you are growing weak. What happens if you become stuck at one point and have no idea on how to remove yourself from the situation? A guard is an action plan for when you get stuck, it will even help you see the barrier before you hit it. A guard will also help you spot danger to your ambitions when danger is near. These barriers and attacks may not always be malicious. When barriers and attacks are not malicious that makes them even harder to see. When you come up with your goal, come up with your guard. Identify the function of the guard and your chances of achieving the goal will rise.

GROUP THINK

It is easy and sometimes feels good to let someone else think for you,

If it sounds good and makes sense, what is said must be true.

Someone who has gained the eye of the public must have the power of critical thinking,

If their name has a doctor in front of it, there must be facts in what they're saying.

This person is extremely angry when giving out information,

If this person is that angry there must be a very good reason.

What is this?

Many more people are following, jumping on the band wagon and agreeing,

The truth has been exposed and all of these people are seeing.

These many people cannot be wrong,

Creating this much of a stir, they will get what they want before long.

I will follow, follow this group until we are in sync,

I will loan control of my mind to the group, this is called group think.

What they believe I believe, what the group says goes,

When the group is angry I am angry, even if the reason nobody knows.

Blind lead the blind I think someone once said,

Let me grab my pitchfork, let me grab my torch, the purpose must be fed.

Have you ever seen a school of fish or maybe a herd of sheep?

When they mimic each other, they are easy to see, control, and lead.

No worries, all is well, the cause is just and great,

It is not like we are spreading lies, disease, and hate.

The group is right and nothing else matters we will do anything,

Arguing with friends, family, and even strangers, the truth is what we bring.

I'll buy merchandise, plane tickets, tune into channels, and give my mind,

To defend our cause, destroy our foes, and protect what is rightfully mine!

Trying to change someone else, is trying to CONTROL someone else, I will be a kind dictator,

My personal world can take a backseat I will deal with my problems later.

Hold on…. I've become something I'm not,

A robot.

When did I become so passionate about an experience I have never had?

When did I become so angry, when did I become so sad?

When did I begin to allow someone else to dictate my actions?

Fear of the unknown, comradery, what is the attraction?

All I wanted was change, all I wanted to do was make a difference,

I watch my "friends" jump off the bridge and I am scared to go the distance.

No, I will not jump the way they told me to,

I will jump, but when I jump, I'll be wearing a parachute.

I may agree, I may disagree, or I may not care,

From this point on I'll think for myself, my mind I will not share.

I will keep my friends if they will have me for who I am today,

If they do not want me to be free we can go our separate ways.

As far as change I need to become the change I want to see,

Taking small steps every day is where I want to be.

Aftermath

It is so easy to fall into a routine that has an agenda you do not agree with. Be sure to remember your own personal values at all times. Your values are your rock to keep you on track to experience life the way your mind perceives it. The moment you abandon your own values because you are not listening to your gut is the moment you are stepping into uncharted waters where anything is possible. As humans we judge everything and we like to believe we have some level of control over our surroundings. We attempt to predict likely circumstances of our actions and that gives us comfort and keeps us in a realm we are familiar with. It is nice to mix up our routines with controlled chaos or random events where we do things we normally wouldn't do. Group think is dangerous because when you wake from the trance you discover that you have done many things that have destroyed the infrastructure you have set up in your life over the years.

FIGHT FOR WHAT YOU WANT

What do you want?

Stop.

Stop.

I did not ask what society wants you to want,

I asked, what do you want?

Take a deep breath, breath in,

Now breath out.

What do you want?

You can have what you want.

Factors, matter, and a formula form,

Calculations begin to flash before your eyes.

The gaps must be filled.

What you do not know you must find out.

Your life is on the line,

Do it now or die inside!

Stuck in a job you do not like,

Stuck with "friends" you do not want.

Shut up and do it,

Change everything.

Change your residence, change your friends, change your job!

Do everything you must do to achieve being you!

Do not let anything hold you back,

Your life is on the line, remember that.

You are greater than you think,

Feel your power, destroy the link.

You are trapped in a reaction to your environment,

Wake up!

Examine your being and see what you think.

Now, you are here, the slate is clean,

It is time.

Tunnel vision, robot mode, receive your self-program.

Dive into the world that you have created.

Mold and shape matter to your desire,

When other programs attempt to enter, burn them with fire.

This is you, everyone else will handle their own,

Don't feel bad, you are not a clone.

Fight for what you want or be consumed,

If you do not fight, regret will be your tomb.

Aftermath

65

The number one thing people express before death (if they have the ability to express anything) is regret. People regret the life they lived because they did not complete or do whatever task there was to complete. While living people may experience depression, loneliness, or low energy due to lack of specific stimulation. The stimulation is whatever makes the individual feel fulfilled. If you are not doing something to stimulate your mind you can feel as if you are the walking dead. A robot programed by society to follow specific orders is how you may feel when you are not doing what your heart desires the most. So, with all this being said, how do you feel? If you knew that your life was on the line would you change your behavior? No matter how many resources you have you cannot be stopped from doing everything in your power to turn your dreams into reality. It is not promised that you will achieve that reality, but you will not find out until you try so go for it.

MY DREAM

I do this for you, I do this for me,

Helping you helps me accomplish my dream.

We are connected, more than life makes it seem,

Helping you helps me accomplish my dream.

When we work together some people call that a team,

Achieving love, peace, and happiness, some call that a dream.

Working with someone else can make you want to scream,

People have personal agendas, they plot, they scheme.

Your happiness fills me with joy, so I will still be on your team,

Helping you helps me accomplish my dream.

I am connected to you, your sorrow may overpower me,

When you cry I cry, I can barely breathe.

I can imagine you being me,

I am not you and so I live without your pain it seems.

I will use my resources to help you, one at a time,

I will eat and you may need to wait for an amount of time.

We may teeter tot until we find balance,

You add your own power to the challenge.

If you ask me why I do what I do,

This is what I will say to you.

I do this for you, I do this for me,

Helping you helps me accomplish my dream.

Aftermath

Has your emotional state ever changed after hearing or watching someone experience something? Some examples of this may include crying while watching a movie, feeling happiness after hearing the story of someone overcoming hardship, or even feeling anger after seeing someone abuse a child. We are connected to each other because we are all human. Our brains are powerful enough to subconsciously have us exchange places with the person of interest. If you watched someone peel the skin off of a nectarine and eat it, would you feel sorry for the nectarine? If you watched someone peel the skin off of a child and eat the child would you feel sorry for the child? Being the same species or even a similar species makes it easy for our brains to connect us to the experiences of others.

This poem is about helping others because you feel their pain and you feel their happiness. My dream is to be surrounded by love, peace, and happiness. I want to help people and share the happiness and joy that I feel every day. Sometimes it is hard to help others because for many reasons they do not trust you but still want your help. Sometimes when you try to help a single person, a mob of people in pain may swarm you for all of your resources. The poem mentions that you may have to eat while the other person waits. To help someone you must be in a state to do so. When spreading the love energy that you have be careful not to be consumed by the pain you are trying to help relieve.

FROM THE AUTHOR

My name is Dewayne Kendrick. This book is one of many gifts I want to give to the world of humans. I have spent my time and life force energy to create this book for you to have. Do what you will, but I have a recommendation on what to do with this book. Use this book, do not simply read it. If anything in this book applies to your life or someone you know, allow it to be a catalyst for change. Every situation is unique to the individual who experiences it. Find a way to heal and grow. I love you because we are connected. Carry on.

www.ingramcontent.com/pod-product-compliance
Lightning Source LLC
Chambersburg PA
CBHW051225250726
48655CB00006B/2600